T0159011

PAIN, PRAYER AND PURPOSE!!

"Seeking A Breakthrough"

Lakisha Jenkins

authorHOUSE®

AuthorHouse™
1663 Liberty Drive
Bloomington, IN 47403
www.authorhouse.com
Phone: 1 (800) 839-8640

Published by AuthorHouse 07/10/2018

ISBN: 978-1-5462-4411-0 (sc)
ISBN: 978-1-5462-4410-3 (e)

Library of Congress Control Number: 2018906378

Print information available on the last page.

TOPICS DISCUSSED

Phase One:

Living with My Grandparents

Going to Live with My Mom

Grandfather's Death

Reunited with My dad

Father's Death

Separation, Insecurities and Self-esteem Issues

Phase One

As a young girl being raised in South Carolina in a small city called Saluda by my grandparents who instilled in me much guidance, morals and respect plays a huge role of the person I am today. My grandparents were family oriented and modeled a very spiritual life. They depended on GOD no matter what the circumstance was. In their home GOD always came first. No matter what trials came about they never stop trusting GOD. I smile as I can remember smelling the early morning breakfast as we gathered to the table for breakfast. This was a daily habit of the family. Also seeing my grandfather take on the role as the provider of the family was very important. He did whatever he had to as a responsible man to make sure his family had a sense of security. Growing up I always hoped to find a man with my grandfather character. My grandmother didn't work. She took care of home and made sure I was taken care of before and after school every day. My grandmother often joked how she got arthritis due to us standing in the cold many morning waiting for the school bus. I'm grateful of all her love and support as a child.

At the age of 13 I wanted to move to Maryland to live with my mom. Things were a bit different. Before this time my only communication with my mom was talking over the phone. With all my older cousins moving away in South Carolina I felt comfortable going to live with her now. My mom had asked me several times to come but I wasn't ready then. My grandfather was very supportive through the process. He often encouraged that I get to know my mom more. My mother worked from home babysitting. She did this for many years before choosing to go outside the house to work. This allowed her enough stability to be home to care for her children and support her family at the same time. In the beginning it was rough getting to know my two younger siblings Carvetta at the time five year's old and Johnisha one year's old and also my mom's boyfriend. My mom's boyfriend's role in the household was different than what my grandfather modeled. I expressed my feelings of him negatively through my behavior. This affected our relationship for several years. As I grew older our relationship became better. I was surprising to see how he still showed love for us after him and my mom relationship ended. He never overlooked us in his future relationships. He didn't believe in the step children title. We were always known as his real children. That is what really caused our relationship to grow. No matter what I needed he was still there. And still today that applies. I can never remember a time he turned me away or said no to anything I asked. My mom as a single mother did face some hard times trying to raise us on her own though. Being the oldest child I had to adjust to helping out more with my sisters. As my mom strived to better our situation things eventually got better. During this time I facing was my own struggle inside with feeling disconnected from my mom. These feelings came from not being raised by her. I let my feelings affect our relationship for a long time. After acknowledging my issues things did get a little better for me. One thing that was similar about the transition of moving with my mom was the spiritual side. Church was a priority in the household. Going to church wasn't an option. It was a must. You went no matter what. I hated having to go to church two to three times a week. It all paid off though. As I got older going to church kept me grounded in many ways. My relationship with GOD today has been a challenge because I was raised in the church and when I felt I wanted to pull away I always found my way back. I'm extremely grateful for the people that stepped in and helped me through my struggles of finding myself. Much thanks to Kimberly and Delbert Pope for displaying the guidance they did for me. Today Kimberly is the BIG SIS I never had. My aunt Linda as well played a huge part of making sure I stayed connected to GOD. Her guidance even now means a lot to me. She is definitely someone I can count on when dealing with any issue. The guidance and time they all took to pour into my life helped tremendously with deciding to turn my life around.

I was dealing with so much inside and just needed the right people to understand my needs. Managing any type of relationship became hard for me. My feelings pertaining to my mom was one thing but not having a relationship with my biological dad as I grew up made it worst. This caused a lot of damage for me and made me very independent as I grew older. My father was incarcerated most of my life. I recall a dream seeing him escorted in chains. We kept in touch through writing and phone calls. Looking forward to his calls and letters was all I had to hold on too. I never saw my dad again until my grandfather passed away and he came to a family gathering. That was in June of 1997. I was 21 years old. That was completely a surprise. Nothing but excitement was written all over my face. We spent every moment possible bonding. It was such a good feeling to also introduce him to his grandson. My oldest son was just one month old. My grandfather never had the pleasure of enjoying this moment. It felt amazing to share this moment with my dad. As we spent time over the next couple days I became very emotional. Before my departure we made plans to stay in touch and spend the holidays together. Unfortunately we never got that chance to do that. My dad passed away 5 months after my grandfather. I was extremely torn apart. It seems he had gotten to a point that he had problems adjusting to everyday life. Some said he often talked about his issues but no one listened or took him serious. I can't even imagine the things he was dealing with inside but it had to be painful. My dad committed suicide one day at work. He was found hanging from a tree in a back field. This was truly heartbreaking to know. My dream of enjoying life with my dad was now over. Now I had lost two valuable men in my life. This left me in a weak spot.

Finding the necessary strength to move forward after both my losses was quite challenging. I now faced the fear of being alone. I was indeed in a lonely place. I was left with a lot of emptiness inside. This caused issues for me in my relationships. No matter how bad a relationship had gotten I stayed due to fear of separation and loneliness. I carried this fear until my late 30's. I'm managing better now in my early 40's.

Many insecurities and self-esteem issues resorted from staying in unhealthy relationships. A year after both deaths I became very promiscuous as well. Searching for the love I had lost from two men that mattered a lot to me. I found myself in a place dealing with men I knew were no good for me. Getting pregnant twice having two abortions. Something I never shared with a lot of people before now. I didn't recognize the damage I was causing for myself. Nothing mattered at that time. In many of my relationships I accepted being mistreated, disrespected and taken advantage of just to feel validated. I've experienced issues of physical, mental and verbal abuse. Plenty of guys saw my weakness and used it to their advantage. At that time I lacked the understanding of self- love, self-worth, self- respect and so much more.

TOPICS DISCUSSED

Phase Two:
My First Love
Our First Child
Relationship Issues
Second Child
Leaving the Relationship
Life with Doug
Our Challenges
Doug's Sickness
Doug's Death
Trusting GOD for Strength

PHASE TWO

My first relationship was with my first love and high school sweetheart. He is the father of both my children. He graduated in 1994 and I graduated in 1995. After we both graduated we continued to date. Two years later we were happy to find out that we were expecting our first child. Shortly after we found out I had miscarried at about 8 weeks. We were both devastated. This is the worst thing any mom wants to experience. That unexpected lost now lead us trying again. And again I miscarried. We tried again for a third time and I also miscarried. Now I'm left to be told by doctors I will never be able to have kids. This was so disturbing to hear. I was left to deal with additional hurt and pain. Depressed and upset. Not understanding why this was happening to me. Finally we just gave up accepting what the doctors had said. Despite my prior losses I was able to give natural birth to our first son Nathaniel DeBerry Jr. He weighed 8lb 10oz and was born on May 23 1997. Proud parents we were. It was a rough pregnancy being considered high risk due to the prior miscarriages requiring a lot of bedrest. I even had to stop working as well. That was a new beginning for us both. It brought forth a lot of responsibilities and a close bond as parents. We later decided to get our own place. Both working we felt we were ready to step out and begin a family together. Things were good for a while but we later faced some difficult moments. One challenge was we both didn't expect for our freedom to be taken away. We both still wanted to hang out and have fun. Without a babysitter that couldn't happen. As Nate Jr. got older my mom started babysitting and I was able to have some fun too. With both us being in our early 20's as parents and not ready to adjust as needed as a team that was our downfall. We still remained together but only for our son. When our differences came about I would take my son and go to my mom's to stay. It was convenient to do but unhealthy for the relationship. Breaking up making up began a cycle for repeated years leading to the birth of our second son Keyshaun.

Keyshaun was born on January 5, 2001. He was born through natural labor and full term as well. Keyshaun weighted 6lbs 12ozs. My pregnancy with keyshaun was a little difficult due to depression issues. Again I was put on bed rest not able to work. No longer working and back home with my mom for support. Dealing with unresolved issues I found myself moving from house to house throughout most of my pregnancy with Keyshaun. Facing some severe complications I did return to my mom's house until I got stable with everything after giving birth. Now also facing paternity issues with their dad things wasn't the best between us. However after that issue was resolved we decided to get back together again. Again we managed well for a short time but couldn't work through the challenges like before. As much as I wanted my kids to be raised by both of us together I had gotten tired and made my mind up I was finally going to leave. March of 2005 I gained enough strength to leave not even knowing where my support was going to come from. Before leaving I shared my thoughts with their dad. He replied stating no other man would ever take me serious enough especially with two kids that wasn't theirs. He was proven wrong shortly after that.

In the midst of facing problems with my children's father I met a man named Doug. It was sometime around November 1998. Doug was a frequent customer at my job and asked for my phone number one day. Starting out as friends we later began dating. I was attracted to him a lot though. He was a good listener and cared enough to recognize the negative effects of my lifestyle and help me understand the importance of bettering myself. We were also both Libras with birthday's only two days apart. We were alike in many ways. Plus he was raised in the south just like me. Doug was my need of comfort especially with the issues I faced issues with my children's father. By him having military background he was more disciplined than me. I loved everything about him. Everything seemed so right with him. It felt good to be with a man I could now confide in. He listened to me and in return gave me advice. He expressed his true thoughts even if it would hurt me to face reality. Doug became very aware of my self-issues and knew the reason why. He always encouraged me to do better no matter what. This helped with realizing I needed to make some changes. Now I was beginning to understand things on a different level. I don't regret making the decision I made. Yes it was rough for a bit but well worth it. I'm thankful for my best friend Cherlyn who opened her home to us for a while. So did my step father and his girlfriend. Afterwards I relocated in Anne Arundel County moving with Doug. Prior to moving in with Doug things were overwhelming. At times I couldn't afford daycare and took my kids to work. They sat in my office for eight hours straight many days. This lead to other issues of course and I just decided to resign with so much going on. Now living with Doug I was starting a new life. Being reminded in many ways of my grandfather by him I became even more attached. I felt extreme closeness with him. I was now with a man who accepted me and my kids. Something their dad said was impossible. I had no money no job nothing. Doug provided everything for us. It felt good to have a man care that much about me. We established a plan to build together. With my kids still being quite young we agreed that is was ok for me to stay at home to avoid worrying about daycare expenses. For a while I stayed home but began working in August of 2009. I was offered a part time job with Anne Arundel County Health Department through the school board which was perfect for me. I worked according to my children school calendar. When school was out I didn't have to work. I couldn't ask for anything better. I didn't have to worry about contributing a big portion towards the bills. Doug took care most of the household responsibilities. I helped with things like small household needs (groceries etc.), and the boy's needs. Things were going great for us.

My passion today to work with young ladies was formed through this job. I connected with so many middle and high school students who were facing all types of family issues. Taking the time to get to know and understand their challenges now lead me in a place of wanting to give back and pour into them. Something I was blessed to have through my challenges as a youth. Becoming dedicated and going out the way formed the relationship I have with my God daughter Adrianna. Adrianna was 14 years old when we first met at Meade Middle School. She would often speak and we became close and connected by her sharing some of her personal challenges. Adrianna had had an abortion. This really troubled her. After getting the abortion she had some unanswered questions about some concerns and I tried to guide her towards some point of understanding. My guidance and support caused her to think of me as a second mom and today she is definitely the daughter I never had.

The year of 2008 was a challenging one. One day my good friend Shawn had brought some important factors to mind while visiting our home. She had noticed a discoloration in Doug's eyes. She informed me to have him get a test done on his liver. Immediately I brought this concern to Doug's attention but he didn't look into it right away. Doug was facing some drinking issues due to depression. He had a hard time dealing with the death of close family members and the loss of a good paying job working for NSA in Fort Meade. It was hurtful to see him go thru this. This brought on many trying times for us. One thing that stood out to me though was how he always managed to sober up and still maintain his role as a provider. Constantly I prayed for him. I needed someone to pray for my strength. It was not at all easy but I felt I owed him this because he was there for me when I had no one. I was scared. This was not the man I had fell in love with. I needed that person back that pushed me to do better and change. The person who helped me during my difficult moment now needed me during his. What was I to do now? Stay and deal with it. Arguments began to start leading to fighting. That's when I called quits. I took my kids and went into a shelter. Eleven years of friendship and now this I asked. We remained in a shelter for several weeks before returning home. It was then Doug had had time to realize and think things over. When I returned he proposed to me. Despite the circumstances I said YES. I felt it was worth a try if we just worked together. We did everything possible to make things work from that point. We started going to church in Baltimore at Empowerment Temple. One of Doug's good friends had invited us to that church one Sunday. The first time we went I had no idea Jamaal Bryant was the pastor. Many days I spent time listening to his sermons both television and online. They were powerful and truly helpful. It was amazing to see him in person. From that point we started to attend church on a regular basis. It was helping us. Doug later began to attend AA meetings and continuing to go see his doctor. He even started working full time again. Things were coming along. Now we could start planning for our wedding. His drinking issue was still there but things were progressing. I was learning ways to support him allowing us to move forward. July 12, 2008 we got married. People that knew about his addiction judged me. I didn't care. Instead I stuck with my decision while praying for change though.

In October 2008 just 3 months after getting married we were informed Doug's liver was failing him. He had cirrhosis of the liver. At this point he needed a liver transplant to live. His condition had taken a turn for the worst. Doug needing a liver transplant meant him sustaining from alcohol totally. Something he had trouble doing. This brought on major issues for him including more and more hospital care visits.

During this time I'm still working at the same job but I was fortunate enough to have a supervisor that cared and understood my situation. Juggling his doctor appointments, being available for his needs, the children needs, working, and maintaining the home was a big task. December of 2008 Doug required full hospitalization. He couldn't function any more at home alone. With him being home it was a bit rough with multi-tasking. I bathe him. I fed him. Wherever he needed to go I took him. I managed to do it all by myself. When his kidneys began to shut down he required additional medical treatment. Eventually he started to experience having seizures. I remember one time I was away from home and the kids called stating Doug had fallen down the steps. Upon arriving and calling for help I had realized he had a seizure. That was scary for us all. Another time we were on our way to my mother's house on 295 south and Doug started seizing in the car. Immediately I had to hurry up and pull over to assist him. When he came to I was able to make it to my moms, drop my kids off and head straight to the nearest hospital. There were times when Doug situation seemed to be getting better only because he had no liquor accessible to him. At home he would hide his alcohol and by the time I found it the bottle would be empty stuffed in the sofa. Prayer still existed within me no matter how things looked. Doctor spoke as if they saw no hope for him. Still I spoke hope. Eventually I just prayed asking GOD to take control and do what's best for him. See with there being such a long time span requiring Doug to sustain from alcohol I knew he would be in the hospital long term. Now being admitted my day consisted of early morning dropping the kids off, heading to work, off work and straight to the hospital not leaving until having to get the boys from daycare. Months went past. Things seemed hopeful. Now Doug needed a surgery. After the surgery he had to remain on life support to survive. Day after day doctors tried to talk me into pulling the plug but I refused. Days later he had begun to make some improvement being able to breathe on his own again but things still turned for the worst. The morning of February 17, 2009 GOD called Doug home. That morning the hospital called to inform me of some complications that started. His blood pressure was starting to decrease. I immediately began to prepare myself. Hours later gathered with family we were informed of Doug death. I remember yelling screaming rolling on the waiting room floor as I digested the news as I waited to go see him. I couldn't comprehend at the time why I kept losing all the males that meant the most to me. Why when things seem to be getting better they are somehow taken from me. Doug death was hard for all of us to manage. My children knew him as their "Poppie". They admired Doug as their stepfather. The man they had grown to establish a deep relationship with. The memories of Doug are remarkable. He loved to laugh and joke. He was a true comedian. Everyone that met him fell in love with him. He had such a great sense of humor. Doug was very outgoing too. To have to accept he was gone and never see him again hurt deeply. To see him lying on that hospital bed not breathing just gone was unbearable. I just couldn't understand how I was going to continue life without him. I had forever lost my soulmate.

Making funeral arrangements was overwhelming. With just a part time income it was impossible. All I can say is GOD worked it all out. I was blessed to have support towards the funeral and burial expenses from his family. I was able to bury my husband nicely. My prayer had been answered. Reflection verse 1 Thessalonians 5:18. In everything thing give thanks: for this is the will of GOD in Christ Jesus concerning you. Day after day bills piled up. A couple months later the house was facing foreclosure. With only being married for about 7 months I wasn't able to seek much help. One thing I did know is GOD wasn't going to let me fall. I trusted GOD to provide for us. Continuing to serve GOD I gained strength to make it through that situation. Believing everything would work out. And it did!!!

TOPICS DISCUSSED

Phase Three:

New Job

New Apartment

Relationship with Ex

PHASE THREE

September 2009 I was blessed with a full time job as a Correctional Officer. GOD had answered my prayer. This was a tremendous increase in pay from my last job. A huge burden was lifted. The house was no longer in foreclosure status but now in the process to be sold. Seven months of not knowing how we were going to survive GOD took care of each and every need. In the beginning yes it was difficult. However I knew I had to take a step towards working towards what I needed. From that point on GOD took control. With the house needing some work I was concerned. It was a blessing to have all the contractors agree to wait for payment until the settlement was complete. This had to be GOD. Now all I had to do was begin deciding my plans concerning moving. Through prayer I asked GOD for help within my decision making. Family members suggested I move back to PG County to have help with the boys. I truly needed that. So my process began with applying for apartments in PG County. Making the step of having to support my boys alone was quite scary. Years ago I had faced so much trying to do things on my own. Even still I knew if I received the blessing then it must be meant. Applying for my first apartment alone I was approved. It was a two bedroom and a den for just $930.00. The price was just within my budget. This was just what I needed. Wait there is more. I had absolutely no security deposit at all. All I needed to do was pick a date, get the keys and move- in. Reflection verse Philippians 4:6 Be careful for nothing; but in everything by prayer and supplication with thanksgiving let your requests be made known unto GOD. MY GOD. MY GOD. Immediately I gave all GOD thanks. The more I prayed and dedicated myself to him he continued to allow the blessings to come. This all worked out just in time for the house to be sold. I was extremely grateful and excited about the new job and new apartment but not ready to start this new phase of my life alone. See at this time I was still fighting depression. It was hard to manage at times. I fought through it though. Day by day I got stronger. Nothing could take away the pain I was feeling inside. The loneliness I felt was unbearable. Many days I cried still not understanding why Doug had to leave me. I tried to find comfort in believing that GOD makes no mistakes. Reflection verse Matthew 11:28 Come unto me, all ye that labour and are heavy laden, and I will give you rest. Many days I spent moments just starring at his pictures talking to him releasing my feelings. I remember sitting in the living room one day dozing off. All of a sudden I begin to hear his voice coming from upstairs calling my name. This was so scary. Through everything I have learned how to encourage myself. Being strong was becoming hard to manage. It helped to realize that even though Doug was absent in body he was present through spirit. This was definitely a hard process to overcome. Fighting the loneliness was difficult. I struggled with my feelings of not having anyone to make me feel loved or accepted. Dealing with these feelings my solution became to start dating too early. Deep inside I knew I wasn't ready. It just seemed right to do to fill that void and emptiness at that time. Making that mistake placed me in a vulnerable position.

Almost a year later I had met a gentleman. He was intelligent, respectful, and hardworking and seemed to have understood all I was dealing with. I adored his great sense of humor and laughter. We started spending time together which led to a relationship in January 2010. The feeling of no longer feeling alone was lovely. Recently during my moments of loneliness I would pray that GOD send me someone with understanding of my previous situation. I felt I had found that. Only for trust issues within me began to develop. Since a young age I had carried self-esteem and insecurities issues I never properly dealt with. When Doug and I was together he introduced me to new things to help me recognize my beauty. He showed me a sexy and classy way of style. I went from wearing tennis shoes and jeans all the time to dressing nicely showing off the little shape I had. That was a start toward gaining confidence in me. After that I decided to wear make-up. This was something that was helped my esteem. Doug was very supportive with understanding my need to feel good about me. Now later on in this relationship I was better in this area but felt as though I was still missing something. I had not yet learned how to love me first. As time passed things did get a bit rough for us. More trust issues. We both were dealing with some type of insecurity and self-esteem problem. I felt he had a problem with commitment and being loyal. We were barely holding on to the relationship. Still I stayed afraid of being alone. I allowed almost anything just to avoid him leaving me. Before I knew it 5 years had gone by. Facing some stressful situations I began to feel neglected by the man I had fell in love with. Often feeling he overlooked my needs. This caused a bit of damage for me. I knew I deserved more. I had recognized my faults but didn't understand my self-worth at that time. This motivated me for once to do something I never did before. Learn how to love myself. Looking for it in men just wasn't working for me anymore.

Around May 2014 I began moving forward ready to love myself, respect myself entirely, and become capable of learning my true self-worth. My whole perspective had changed. I began to think about how GOD was the only one capable of showing me true compassionate love. Today I thank GOD for bringing forth that bad relationship because it forced me to grow into a much better person. GOD literally had to show me what wasn't for me. I ask him to show me and he did. Reflection verse: James 1:5 If any of you lack wisdom, let him ask GOD, that giveth to all men liberally, and upbraidth not; and it shall be given him. Time after time I was willing to stay in an unhealthy relationship. I was able to forgive even though I was hurting. Now moving forward I was tired of that and needed to apply my faith and gain understanding to do what was best for me. I finally faced my fears of being alone. With such a huge challenge in front of me I started to reflect on past situations GOD has brought me through. In 2011 the transmission in my minivan at the time had went bad and I was left with no transportation at all. I was completely worried because I had no savings at all going forward. It was definite that I get some sort of transportation because I worked far from home at night. A suggestion was made by my best friend to try to apply for a Navy Federal car loan. At the time I questioned if I should do it. I couldn't see how I was going to fit a car note in my budget. Still debating I applied. In less than 24 hours I was approved for a 18,000 car loan. Again I was blessed. Two days later I was able to purchase my first car. A 2011 Dodge Caliber with only 1056 miles on it. May I add again no down payment required. That car payment adjusted well within my budget too. I still own that car today. No repossessions. I was always able to pay as required. Won't he do it? Reflection verse Luke 1:37 For with GOD nothing shall be impossible.

TOPICS DISCUSSED

Phase Four:

Gaining More Faith

Reunited as a Family

Keyshaun Behavior Challenges

Facing Financial Difficulties

Financial Turnaround

PHASE FOUR

Recapping some struggles of the past and knowing that GOD had allowed things to work out helped me to become stronger in trusting him completely. Just as the car situation I previously spoke of.

In 2006 my family was so divided. My mom was living one place. Both of my sisters were living somewhere else. Living further away our family communication wasn't the best. I would constantly pray that GOD would reconnect us all. Asking him to restore all damage and hurt each of us was dealing with. As a family we were faced with our own separate issues and we lost track as a family. Knowing all that my mom was facing I prayed that one day she would gain enough strength to get back on her feet. About a year later GOD started working in that situation. I received a call one day from my mom asking me to come get her. She no longer felt like dealing with the things she had to deal with living with someone else. From that moment she moved forward never looking back. Shortly afterwards Carvetta and I began to reconnect again. We had lost contact. Now all we needed was for Johnisha to be reunited. Two years later that happens for her. My mom and sisters shortly after was able to get a place of their own. To look back and realized how GOD answered my prayers truly reminds me of how good he is. Just like any other family we still have differences but going thru that situation really made us realize how important family really is.

I was dealing with my own problems regarding Keyshaun being diagnosed with adhd, bipolar and depression at the age of 10. This was definitely a trying experience at first in which required much prayer. Reflection verse James 5:14 This is the confidence we have in approaching GOD: that if we ask anything according to his will, he hears us. Keyshaun had severe periods of expressing anger. Dealing with this situation alone was severely overwhelming at times. With so many other responsibilities it took all of me to stay strong. At times I questioned GOD why me. But after recapping the scripture Proverbs 3:5-6 Trust in the Lord with all thine heart; and lean not unto thine own understanding. In all thy ways acknowledge him, and he shall direct thy paths I seemed to find some comfort. I became stronger with accepting the situations I was faced with depending on GOD for guidance to get through them. Finding time for counseling, doctor visits and school meeting was a true task. I found a way to manage things though. Then more problems came. In 2015,

Keyshaun had started facing issues with the Juvenile System. Then now being told he was struggling with ODD instead of bipolar. A big part of Keyshaun challenges seemed to have been his choice of friends that were impacting his influence of going down the wrong path. I often took time to explain to him how his decisions were affecting his life. As a mom you fear getting that devastating phone call one day saying something has happened to your child. You fear the thought of thinking one day your son will end up in jail. Even still I never stop praying for my son though. I believed GOD still has a plan for his life. Change is never impossible for anyone. Being a Correctional Officer it has helped me to establish the importance of never giving up on your child. I would hear so many stories from inmates of the young generation that came from dysfunctional families. Some came from broken homes. Some had no guidance or role model. Others parents had given up on them. Parents who were struggling with some type of addiction and they have no one. Being a Correctional Officer has also taught me patience and tolerance that helps me in my everyday life. I'm grateful of the knowledge I have gained through my job. If we pray for guidance and direction GOD he will give us just that. Through prayer I received a vision for my life. Deciding to write this book was a part of a vision Pastor Wayne Howden a coworker of mine while working in the school system stated and prophesized over my life during a time of comforting during my husband's death. He spoke how he one day saw me writing a book and helping women of all kinds gain strength and also being an encouragement to them as well through my struggles. I ignored the thought at first but somehow the thought still lingered around for years. When I began to examine my life of my experiences and what it took for me to find strength to press my way through situation I was motivated to share my story. I've gained a huge passion to encourage through all my troubles. Many times I've prayed asking GOD to direct my path making me available to share with others to be a blessing. I knew this was for me I just had to continue to trust GOD to lead me in the right direction to find the right guidance to help me understand my purpose in life. Remaining patient I received a blessing in February of 2015. I was given a book to read by a coworker after sharing my passion for women ministry. The book was called LIFE AFTER THE SILENCE: FROM PAIN TO POWER TO PURPOSE by Angela D. Wharton. This book helped me to understand some of the things I was confused with regarding my thoughts of where to begin. I'm not one to read that often and I read this book in two days. This was helpful to me because I started the year off committing myself to finally write a book not even knowing where to start. After reading this book I was now ready to develop an outline of my book. I spent time brainstorming my key areas. That's when I officially put all my thoughts together on paper.

Back in August of 2013 I was faced with some financial struggles that lead to me losing my apartment and needing to move in with family it was difficult to completely rely on my faith. Pressing my way I still prayed and believed things would get better. For 9 months I did everything necessary to make a difference because I felt I had failed my kids who looked up to me every day. Needing to rebuild and repair my credit I developed a plan to work overtime every chance I was able to. I saved money to pay off creditors hoping to receive settlement offers. And that I did receive. My time frame needing to stay with family was about a year. Needing an apartment sooner I took a chance to applying for an apartment earlier than expected. The first place I tried I was disappointed because I was denied. Shortly after that I tried at a different location and I was accepted. I was now about to move into my own two bedroom apartment. Originally my significant other at the time that I talked about previously had planned to move with us. He later changed his mind and I was left debating on whether to still move by myself. I just wasn't sure I could afford it on my income alone. The rent was much higher than I had ever paid. Feeling completely lost of what to do I talked it over with my best friend Cherlyn. She encouraged me to still move and trust GOD to provide no matter how things seemed. I trusted GOD before and he came through so I didn't understand why I was so nervous now. As suggested I stepped out on faith in a way I never had before. I accepted the apartment. Still not knowing how I was going to get the money needed for the security deposit. I stopped worrying myself and prayed. Reflection verse Mark 11:24 Therefore I say unto you, what things so ever ye desire, when ye pray, believe that ye receive them, and ye shall have them. My next paycheck was over 1600.00. That was more than enough needed to move and get situated with things. Here's the thing when I was working that overtime I had no plans on moving at that time. Just to add my kids didn't even have to change their school. Truly no one but GOD allowed this to work out just as I needed. I knew I would be blessed for my faithfulness. I pressed my way through depression. Still remembering how he worked out so many others situations before this. So I just kept praying. Reflection verse 1Chronicles 16:11 Look to the Lord and his strength; seek his face always. That year brought the real meaning of stepping out on faith. Not once did my lights get cut off. Not once did we starve for food or go without what we needed. GOD truly looked out for us. My faith during such a time was beginning of discipline for me to realize I can't make it without GOD. Every experience brought a lesson. When you pay close attention and adhere to the order of which things happen in your life it can cause you to gain understanding of what he is trying to do in your life. That's how I could now encourage myself when no one else is around to encourage me. GOD knows what we all need. In what timing we all need things. And he grants everything we need at the right time. If we just continue to trust him like amazing things will begin to happen in our lives. After this experience my spiritual life began to improve for the better. I was maturing growing and beginning to establish a better relationship with GOD. Not always able to attend church at the time. However I put forth much effort to stay connected to GOD. My prayer life had become more intense. No matter what the issue was I prayed about it. I recall the day I heard Steve Harvey share on his radio station how important it was to end your prayer saying Lord According to you will. Reflection verse Romans 8:28 For we know all things work together for good to them that love GOD, to them who are called according to his will. From that day forward I have always spoke those words in my prayer and I began to see CHANGE. Through change brought motivation which brought determination. I have no plans on turning back. GOD is showing me a different way of thinking. I'm excited about my future and ready to receive all he has for me.

TOPICS DISCUSSED

Phase Five:

Rebuilding Relationships with Family

Prayer for Financial Help

More Challenges with Keyshaun

Oldest Son Become Employed

Issues with Feeling Lonely

PHASE FIVE

May 2014 learning how to value any type of relationships was something I learned through my experiences. At one time in my life when disagreements and conflicts came I didn't care what happen going forward. As I became more spiritually in tuned with GOD my perspective changed of how to handle any type relationship. Rebuilding the relationship with my mother and sisters was valuable to me. Our past issues were hard to let go of but I knew I needed to forgive. In order to move forward this was required of me. GOD uses all kinds of situations to get our attention on recognizing the need of forgiveness. I believe GOD used the time I stayed with them as a outlook for me. It amazed me to see how GOD had begun to work through the circumstances with Keyshaun to re-establish me and Carvetta's relationship. See she had once faced similar situations as a youth that keyshaun was currently dealing with. As a youth she was put out of PG county schools also being sent away for several years before returning home. She shared with me how she wished she had done better then. How it would hurt her to see her nephew make the same mistakes as she did. That alone was our way of beginning to build the communication needed as sisters. In the past my mom and I bumped heads a lot. It wasn't until after I moved out that I began to acknowledge our issues. Being ready to address my feelings finally. It took time but we finally managed. Because I had been holding so much inside regarding my mom I was claiming to release every bit of it and finally let go. Also struggling inside with extreme hurt, pain, and disappointment that I felt from my last relationship was a challenge for me. My heart was destroyed and finding a way to forgive him didn't seem possible. It was a long process that ended up being a complete road towards growth. A year later I found myself in a place now ready to forgive him. My most effective relationship has always been the one I've had with my best friend Cherlyn. We have been friends for over two decades now. She has been there during the good and the bad. When I felt alone she was there. Whenever I needed a listening ear she was there. She has encouraged me when I didn't believe in myself. It was her that challenged me to take that one step toward faith when I doubted GOD the most. Her exact words were "Kisha you got to step out on faith and trust GOD". I'm so appreciative of our friendship. Nothing in my life is and ever will be perfect. Things are definitely better though. And all it took was to let go and let GOD.

After doing well with rebuilding relationships I then choose to focus more on my finances. Being blessed to have a place to call my own my goal now was to try to become more stable financially. I constantly prayed asking GOD for help. Not knowing how I would receive the help I believed it would happen. Bills became overwhelming. Depression sat in not being able to do much for me and my kids. Nothing big just a nice vacation or getaway would had been nice to enjoy. Nathaniel was 17 and working his first job. As he saw me struggling to keep things together he offered to help in any way he could. I was grateful of any help from him. This was such a blessing. I remember him saying as a child "Ma if I could get a job I would help you." Well I must say he kept his promise. I was amazed of how responsible he had become. GOD used my son in the form of a blessing in the time of our need.

Still left to face some issues concerning Keyshaun I kept going. Already dealing with the Juvenile System we had issues at home and at school. He was arrested at gun point. Taken into custody and questioned by the police. At the age fourteen Keyshaun was put on house arrest for a short time. The judge ordered two stet dockets for him to stay out of trouble and community service. Still I prayed. Already dealing with his Adhd, ODD, and depression concerns it was quite stressful. Many times I wished I had a companion for support. Keyshaun's father wasn't involved in his life due to his behavior issues. I needed someone to release my thoughts, tears, and heart too. Carrying all I was facing built up emotions of loneliness. Many nights I cried myself to sleep. At times it was depressing to look at couples appearing to be happy. Wondering what was holding me back from finding true companion. It was that serious for me. I knew I was much stronger than that. It took a lot of time to adjust to accepting be single for once in my life. Almost all my life I was either with or seeing someone. Now wanting to not go back to what felt right but finding strength to do what was right was my focus. This was truly a hard adjustment. Continuing to focus on me I was introduced to someone by my good friend Shawn sometime later down the line. A bit stronger this time with my guards up I gave it a chance. We became good friends over time. With me puzzling with my thoughts about my ex he shared things from a man's point of view. Something we women don't pay attention to. He helped me recognize some key factors of both our mistakes. His encouraging words gave me additional motivation to continue learning me. A lot of things stood out about him. He was caring and respectful. I could talk to him about anything. I was impressed by his relationship with his kids. Keeping in mind we could never establish anything together because he was already married. Not happily married he said but not willing to leave his kids either. As he began to share some things about his life I took him seriously. From day one he was honest and I respected that about him. This was the first time a man was honest about his situation giving me the option to accept my place. We both knew the chances of becoming deeper involved. Feelings were expressed and things became quite challenged for me. I was drawn to the way he delivered his thoughts. He was not a person to argue. That was helping me to work on the emotions and expressing them correctly. I failed at this in my last relationship. Even in this situation I prayed to GOD about my feelings for a married man. I wasn't proud of myself. It all just felt good at the time. Through a lot of continued prayer I was able to maintain myself and make it past the challenges positioning myself right where I needed to be. This encounter was helpful because it challenged me in my weak area as far as given in to any man just to feel accepted. In my prior relationship my way of thinking was not stable and it affected me in various ways. Now I was in a place of gaining some sort of redirection. This experience has taught me how to recognize and set limitations for myself to avoid being hurt again. He was a great support during a difficult moment in my life. I was able to seek the necessary understanding and knowledge of men to help me move forward and determine better standards for myself. Understanding I didn't have to sleep with every man I met either. Later on I recognized this situation as a test to see how much I truly wanted to keep pursuing in the right direction. I wanted better for myself this time around. I desired to find someone who seemed right in the spiritual area as well. This was important this time around. I desired someone who was driven towards their dreams and wanted to build together. I certainly understand I want find the perfect man but I do hope to find someone who understands things on the same level I do. When I commit to someone I do it without limitations. Sometimes I think I give too much. Through prayer hopefully one day I will understand this concept a little better. I just want to be loved in return without any limits...

TOPICS DISCUSSED

Phase Six:

Learning to Love Me First

Creating a Plan

Nate Graduation

Passion for Ministry

Seeking Change through Fasting

Phase Six

Making the decision to love me first was the best decision I ever made for myself. And until this day it continues to be my focus. My struggle for many years with depression from situation to situation has truly shown me my true strength. As I found myself pushing through each circumstance desiring to share and encourage others it brought out another side of me. I became more social. I stayed to myself a lot not really being a people person. The adjustment of dealing with my inner self had now positioned me in a place letting go of keeping myself so closed in. I take depression serious and plan to always do my best to continue to press through the trying times. Through this experience I've gained a lot of confidence. Learning to interact with other people than my family and close friends has shown me a lot. It's exciting to realize my past frame of mind before now. I'm now more social and will say Hello to someone first. This was not me before at all. Something so small has taught me a lot the changes needed in us first before dealing with others. Being able to create a plan and better understand my needs has helped me in many ways. Not just for myself but my children as well. Nathaniel last year of high school I was faced with a lot. It was challenging to stay and remain focused no matter what was going on around me. I needed him to succeed and continue to strive towards his goals. And he was doing just that. Managing day school, night school, and a part-time job he dedicated his all. I was grateful for the opportunity to see him walk across the stage on May 19, 2015. Being able to celebrate his success was quite emotional. With family by our side full excitement we all shared. Not just for his graduation but also because in 4 days after this he would also be celebrating his 18th birthday as well. All my sacrifices as a single mom had now paid off. As a graduate and a young man he was offered a management position with only being employed for about 6 months. As I watched how motivated he was it brought back memories when I was his age doing the same thing working in management as well. With so much going on it was difficult to fit time in towards my passion. Wanting to encourage and share with women of all ages. I spent a few months sorting out my thoughts and establishing key areas I wanted to address. It was then shortly afterwards that I was then faced with more concerns regarding Keyshaun behavior. He was staying out late at night. He showed extreme anger at times. Not attending school and much more. Now only left to struggle with depression again. Managing things alone was very overwhelming I became frustrated every time I saw my boys fight. Nathaniel played the role as needed as the older brother correcting keyshaun of his behavior but that only lead to additional issues in the household. Sometimes assistance from the police was necessary. To help eliminate some of my stress Keyshaun went to stay with his aunt Carvetta. During this time I had begun to reach out to several resources requesting help but was unsuccessful. With Keyshaun also having pending court concerns I was concerned about his future. When people spoke negative about him I understood my son challenges and why. He had a hunger from not having his father in his life. I began to go into deep prayer kneel at the foot of my bed. I prayed with tears running down my face asking GOD for help and deliverance for my child. I was scared and feared the worst for him. July of 2015 I began a 30 days fast to be released of the things that became so frustrated to manage. A month later I decided to attend therapy to help gain a positive approach of dealing with my frustration. Feeling overwhelmed with all the things going on I wanted to understand what I was doing wrong as a parent. Our communication was completely broken. He wanted to do whatever he wanted and I wasn't allowing that in my house. So he acted out more. Today I'm glad I was mature of a parent to seek help through therapy. It was a extreme help with a new beginning for us. Afterwards I was able to learn helpful strategies with dealing with my frustration and depression.

Keyshaun and I was able to build our communication again and move forward. A short time afterwards Keyshaun began to play football. This was a huge motivator for him. Football was his first love. Football kept him busy and out the streets as well. Overtime I began to notice some improvement in his overall behavior too. I was exciting to hear him say "I love you ma" more often. Being around so many positive male figures that knew his challenges and still showed they cared about him was a positive break for him. They saw his potential despite his current actions. They wanted the best for him like I did. Keyshaun's father had a hard time accepting his challenges and realizing how important his presence in his son life meant. I was grateful for the financial blessing to have even been able to even afford being able to pay for football. A payment plan was offered because I was able to pay all at once. In additional his coach offered to help out with transportation issues. By me working at night it was difficult to do it all. To show how much I appreciated his help I gave him gas as a way of thanking him. At this time I was facing more extreme financial conditions. With already struggling financially it was quite rough. Sometimes it was stressful trying to balance out money for lunch and other needs. It all worked out for the best. As I attended his games many mornings just getting off at 6am getting little or no sleep I was so proud of my son. He was giving football his all. Being able to play both running back and safety he mastered it. Keyshaun was full of speed and unstoppable. This brought back memories of when he played in 2009 for GORC Football in Anne Arundel County. He was chosen for the Select Team his first year. That's how I knew my boy had skills. So now looking forward seeing him score touchdowns, tackles and run with extreme speed was a tremendous blessing. Every game I made sure I made it known #10 was my son. Even as he faced injuries he was still willing to be dedicated to winning. Keyshaun showed total commitment to football. He was a team player among his team mates as well. His biggest dream was to become a NLF player one day. With so many other highlights football was beginning to shift and redirect Keyshaun in the direction he needed to go. Most importantly he was at the stage of forming his own relationship with GOD. Keyshaun had started attending church on his own with one of his close friends. GOD was indeed answering yet another prayer. Things finally seemed to progress for once.

TOPICS DISCUSSED

Phase Seven:
Starting to Date Again
Dating a New Guy
Morning of 10/19/16
Dealing with Guilt and Shame
Final Thoughts

PHASE SEVEN

With everything seeming to be going well and improving I now felt I had reached a place where I would be comfortable dating again. With my progress and growth past my recent relationship and know understanding and loving me I felt I was in a better place in that area. Beginning to start over with a new way of thinking not feeling the need of validation or acceptance of a man for the first time was a huge improvement for me. I began the process of meeting people and it was quite interesting. Some men I met I had absolutely no interest in at all. Some knowing all they wanted was sex I turned away. And some being willing to provide with the exchange of sex I declined. Some men stood out but they never showed enough interest. They never called just text all the time. Some would only to call at night. I desired more than that. Online dating became an option for me. Again some seeming ok and others not ok. Then one day I received a message from this one guy. As we began to communicate and talk I was able to recognize we had things in common. He was 8 years older than me. We got along great and we responded well towards one another. He always called. Showed he was interested in me. Our communication was good. He had no problem taking me out and paying for the meal. He had a job and seemed to be a hard worker. He expressed his future goals and adjustments in life in he felt he needed to make. Things were ok at first. Only to later found out this man had some health concerns requiring him to be admitted in the hospital for a short time. Medically he was dealing with a heart problem. I was even more surprised to find out he had now become homeless too. Totally shocked and stuck in my thoughts because he was hiding it well. Not wanting to turn away I decided to still be involved and support him. I would allow him the time to take showers at my home and give him something to eat. When weather conditions got terrible cold or raining I allowed him to stay at home. Truly not an easy decision but something inside would not allow me to let him sleep on the street. Prior to this we would talk about where he was going sleep that night. He would think about which subway station he could get away with resting for a few hours. What train he was going to try to ride most of the night. This was completely uncomfortable. So yes I agreed to help him out temporarily until he found a place of his own. Also having the opportunity to talk to his mom about a few things in the beginning helped with my overall decisions too. Plus I was not trying to judge him off his past. He had previously expressed the need of wanting to do better. So I was willing to assist him in any way I could. He was constantly searching for better job offers. He also desired to get to know GOD more. The one reason he felt his past relationships had failed. Not being spiritually connected. Knowing all that I felt he was a decent person. Things were going good at first. Then moments came where he shared his thoughts of fear of dying. He expressed his feelings regarding his lack of communication with family and why. Not feeling loved at all. He struggled with getting beyond his past. With all this I could now realize his lack of love for himself. Previously having to deal with this myself to now being in a place where I love myself more I felt I could help him love him as well. I was wrong. At that time I didn't completely understand that self-love has to be recognized from within first. In addition to the things I just mention overtime he began to show jealously, trust issues, anger issues and later I was informed of his mental issues as well. I was now frustrated by his actions. I would listen still puzzled inside because I wanted to end things. My biggest challenge with him was his filthy mouth when he became angry. Then he would apologize afterwards. I was completely turned off. Even still I did my best to refrain from responding to him in the same manner. I realize he was hurt and probably wanted me to feel hurt as well. He would use things I had shared with him about my past against me. Never would I continue to except this from a man. So I began to space myself. Not really entertaining his actions. He now felt rejected by me. I knew I had to remain determined to continue to face my own self-issues and continuing to be involved with him was beginning to break my focus and strength. I was still willing to help him but not be involved with him acting this way. It was when he started drinking that I just could not deal with. I had lost my husband due to drinking and depression. This was a sensitive factor for me. Time went on he continued to look for a place but nothing came through. I recall listening to a conversation he had with a family member. It appeared he had asked to go stay with them but they said no. He seemed very disappointed and became upset. Once that happen I tried to gain a bit more patience but it was difficult. The morning of 10/19/16 is where things turned for the worse. After dealing with so much previously and the current disrespect thru phone conversations and texts I had to let go to keep me together. That morning I asked him to leave my home for good. He had disrespected me to the highest level. He refused becoming angry and disrespectful. He was loud enough to get both my boys attention. This immediately turned into a domestic dispute. He assaulted both my boys. Stabbing first Nate Jr in the arm and then afterwards stabbing Keyshaun in the chest. Keyshaun did not survive his injury to the heart. During that tragic moment I blacked out for a moment. Seeing him with a knife in his hand aiming it at me and my boys was terrifying. My mind was racing with so many thoughts. All I could think about is my boys during that time. Just to have to stand in between my boys and this man during this dispute was so disturbing to me inside. I live everyday struggling with Keyshaun death because I was willing to help someone and lost my son in the midst of doing so. In my head I often relive the moment seeing EMT come to his aid as they stated he was about to go into cardiac arrest as they escorted me out the apartment. I remember the look on his face as he gasped for air. I watched from a short distance as they rushed him to the ambulance. Hours later while being questioned at the police station I was informed Keyshaun didn't survive his injury. That was the most hurtful moment of my life. Once being united with my family I completely collapsed and needed help from EMT to recover. My blood pressure was high and I could not focus. The days ahead were painful. Somehow I managed to gain strength make it through. Spiritually I was challenged. I truly felt like giving up. It was a moment of being on the edge of losing me. Many days I felt guilty and ashamed. I felt ashamed because of my decisions leading up to this. So ashamed I was afraid of leaving my own home. Even for a simple therapy appointment. And feeling guilty about the prayer I prayed months ago asking GOD for some relief from my frustration I was carrying inside. Inside I felt I was such an awful mother for allowing this to happen to my child. It took time, support, and encouragement to get past blaming myself. Many nights I cried not being able to sleep. I knew I needed GODs help to make it through. Each day I was fighting to survive. I was judged by many who didn't even understand me or the situation. Having to deal with news reports, videos being made about me and social media alone was a lot to carry. I pressed forward anyway. I somewhat found comfort knowing I had took the time to discuss my decisions of letting him come stay with my oldest son first. And that it was not as people thought that I put a man before my kids. I shared my reasons for the decisions with my son as well. I remember watching Joyce Meyers speak on a message about being willing to love based on a person potential. She began to explain the negative points of which all I hadn't even realized before this experience. Being able to hear her explain the concept of having a "false sense of responsibility" meaning you feel the need to take on someone else problems. Oh how this spoke volume into me. That's what I did. Took on his situation fully and accepted things based on his potential I felt he had. That message was such an encouragement to me. It allowed me to pay more attention to the decisions I made and think about them more clearly. I'm no longer quick to own other people problems. Today I am more cautious of my decisions. I evaluate men on a different level as well. I've had to press my way through a lot of hurt, pain and disappointment. I even reached the point of forgiving this man for taking my son's life. Not feeling validated to prove or explain anything to anyone. I'm continuing to gain strength through therapy, family support and church. I'm determined to not let this circumstance cause me to give up on life. I try my hardest to push through the dark moments and never doubt that GOD. I've been able to finish this book entirely June of 2017 with a better mindset as before in every area of my life. Understanding that all I can do is put my trust in GOD for complete strength and deliverance. Why it took this and maybe other painful situations to get here I have no idea. I just continue to thank GOD I made it through each and every battle, struggle, circumstance and situation that tried to get the best of me. I'm striving more each day to develop a more positive stand point when facing challenges. I've learned a dark moment don't have to remain dark. It all depends on YOU. Whether or not you can adjust to get to place where you need to be to get your life back in order. For once in my life I feel something I never have before. And that's PURPOSE!!!!!

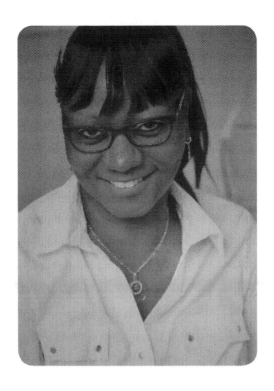

About the Author

Lakisha Jenkins was raised in South Carolina until the age of 14. She then moved to Maryland. Lakisha is the oldest of three siblings. Lakisha has three children. Nathaniel who is 21 years old, Keyshaun who passed away at the age of 14 in 2015 and D' Andre 1 years old. Every day she strives to be a good role model for her family. Lakisha has faced many difficult challenges in life and did not let them consume her. She has endured many storms from being a single mom, dealing with a behavior challenged son (ODD/ADHD), a series of bad relationships and insecurities. Lakisha's turnaround started when she started to feel abandoned and rejected by men. From that point on she began to want more out of life. Overtime her challenges made her stronger. She has gained a passion to help other women through her own struggles. With GOD's help she has managed to survive them all. Certain moments has definitely made her a stronger person. Losing her grandfather in 1997 was one of them. In which her self-esteem issues began to increase. About three months later the passing of her father occurred. In February of 2009 Lakisha lost her husband just a 7months after becoming married. They had a friendship of over 11years prior to marriage. In October of 2015 she lost her 14yr old son who was assaulted and killed by a man she was dating. This was the hardest grief process she ever had to face. Lakisha survived this lost by forming a better spiritual life. This was an experience that completely destroyed her. Her life has transformed in so many ways. Starting over was extremely difficult for her. Lakisha knows the changes grief takes you through. She has had to push herself even when she didn't understand where she would end up. Increasing her faith is a part of her remaining strong. She has now recognized her level of strength and continues to strive to succeed further in life. Lakisha shares her journey of life in her book "PAIN, PRAYER, AND PURPOSE. A book she hopes to encourage women of all ages. Believing and trusting GOD for brighter moments. While continuing to grieve through her son's death Lakisha formed a Self-Love Ministry in 2016. In January of

2018 she formed a Women's Group (SISTERS UNITED ON PURPOSE) geared to strengthen and empower women dealing with self- challenging circumstances. In April of 2018 Lakisha became a Certified Life Coach. Having now gone through several trying times she hopes to encourage other women to step out of their comfort zone and strive pass any current stronghold they may be facing. Lakisha finds balance in life through her passion of encouraging others. It is also a sense of self therapy as well. She enjoys sharing her story and is indeed an example of a TESTIMONY.

Contact

For bookings/scheduling/inquiries:

Coach Kisha

Email: lovingme1st_selflove@yahoo.com

Phone: 1-800-583-9121

And we know that in all things GOD works for the good of those who love him, who have been called according to his purpose. Romans 8:28

Printed in the United States
By Bookmasters